LORNA DOONE

OXFORD BOOKWORMS LIBRARY

Human Interest

Lorna Doone

Stage 4 (1400 headwords)

Series Editor: Jennifer Bassett
Founder Editor: Tricia Hedge
Activities Editors: Jennifer Bassett and Alison Baxter

R. D. BLACKMORE

Lorna Doone

Retold by
David Penn

Illustrated by
Dylan Gibson

OXFORD UNIVERSITY PRESS

OXFORD

UNIVERSITY PRESS

Great Clarendon Street, Oxford OX2 6DP

Oxford University Press is a department of the University of Oxford.
It furthers the University's objective of excellence in research, scholarship,
and education by publishing worldwide in

Oxford New York

Auckland Cape Town Dar es Salaam Hong Kong Karachi
Kuala Lumpur Madrid Melbourne Mexico City Nairobi
New Delhi Shanghai Taipei Toronto

With offices in

Argentina Austria Brazil Chile Czech Republic France Greece
Guatemala Hungary Italy Japan Poland Portugal Singapore
South Korea Switzerland Thailand Turkey Ukraine Vietnam

OXFORD and OXFORD ENGLISH are registered trade marks of
Oxford University Press in the UK and in certain other countries

ISBN 978 0 19 479177 9

Printed in Hong Kong

Map by: Tim Slade

Word count (main text): 17,000 words

For more information on the Oxford Bookworms Library,
visit www.oup.com/elt/bookworms

CONTENTS

1

The end of school days

I am John Ridd, a farmer of the village of Oare in Somerset, and I have a story to tell you. It is about some things that happened to me in my younger days.

On the 29th November 1673, when I was twelve years old, John Fry, a worker from our family's farm, came to collect me from my school at Tiverton. He rode his horse up to the gate, leading my own little horse behind him. He was two weeks early, so I knew something was wrong.

'What are you doing here, John?' I asked him. 'It's not the holidays yet.'

He would not look at me. 'Oh, I know that, young Master Ridd. But your mother has saved the best apples,

John Fry rode his horse up to the gate.

and cooked some wonderful cakes – all for you.'

'And Father? How is Father?' I said. It was usually Father who came to collect me, and it was strange that John Fry hadn't said anything about him.

'Oh, he's very busy on the farm just now,' he said. But John wasn't his usual self, and I knew this was a lie.

When I had packed my bags and said goodbye to my friends, I got on my horse and we started the journey home.

It was a long journey from Tiverton to Oare, and in places the road was very bad. John Fry still would not tell me why he had come to collect me, or answer my questions about Father. He looked unhappy about something, but I tried to hope for the best, as boys always do.

On the hill at the end of Dulverton town, we saw a big coach with six horses. In the front seat of the coach sat a foreign-looking woman, and next to her was a little dark-haired girl. I could see from the girl's soft skin that she was from a rich family, and I felt too shy to look at her more than once. She didn't look at me at all. Opposite them sat a very beautiful lady, in fashionable clothes, and next to her was a little boy, who was about two or three years old. The woman in the front, I thought, must be the servant of the family. I always remembered the family afterwards, because I had never seen people who were so grand, and so rich.

After Dulverton, the road got worse and worse, and soon we came into a very dangerous part of the country. This was Exmoor, a place of high, wild hills and deep

Next to the woman was a little dark-haired girl.

valleys, and on Exmoor lived a family of robbers called the Doones. Everyone was afraid of them. They had robbed and murdered on Exmoor for many years, and had grown very strong. Now it was getting dark, and a fog was coming down. It was just the kind of night when the Doones would be out – and we were coming near to the path that they always used.

I wanted to ride fast, and cross the Doone path as quickly as possible, but John Fry knew better.

'Go slowly and quietly,' he said, 'if you want to see your home again.'

But when we came to the valley where the Doone path was, we heard the sound of horses.

'Hide!' said John, and we rode our horses off the path, and hid. But I wanted to look at the Doones, and went up onto a hill above the path. From there I saw a frightening sight.

Below me, moving quietly, were thirty horsemen. They were heavy, strong men, like all the Doones, and they were dressed for battle, carrying guns. Tied to their horses were all the things they had stolen. Some had sheep or other animals. But one man had a child across his horse – a little girl. She had on a very expensive dress, and I thought it was probably for this that the Doones had stolen her. I could not see whether she was alive or dead, but the sight of that child made me sad, and angry.

When we got home to the farm, my father did not come out to meet us, not even when the dogs ran up and made a lot of noise. 'Perhaps he has visitors,' I thought, 'and is too busy to come out.' But really I knew this was not true. I went away and hid. I didn't want anyone to tell me anything. I heard my mother and sister crying when they came out to find me, but I could not look at them.

Later they told me everything: my father had been killed. He had been murdered by the Doones.

It happened on his way back from the market at Porlock, on a Saturday evening. He was riding with six other farmers, and the Doones stopped them and asked them for their money. The other farmers passed their money over at once, but my father was brave. He rode at them, waving his long stick above his head. He managed to hit quite a few heads, but one Doone was waiting at the side of the road with a gun, and shot him.

———— •●• ————

Although we knew it was the Doones who had killed my father, it was useless even to ask the local judges or law officers to do anything about it. They were afraid of the robbers, too – or were even helping them. The Doones did almost anything they wanted on Exmoor.

They were not local people. They came from the north of England, where their leader, Sir Ensor Doone, had been a rich man, with a lot of land. But he argued with his cousin, the Earl of Lorne, who had even more land, and because of the trouble he caused, the King took away nearly everything that Sir Ensor owned. A proud, angry man, Sir Ensor refused to make peace with his cousin, and without his land and farms he became very poor. Then he found that people who had once been happy to know him now turned away from him.

After this, Sir Ensor lived his life outside the law. With his wife and family and a few servants, he looked all over the country for a place to live, where no one would know him, and he could start again. He chose Exmoor, where few people live, and found the perfect place to build a new home.

This was the place we now call Doone valley. It is a green valley far from any town, surrounded by steep, rocky mountains. At first Sir Ensor lived peacefully, and the local people were friendly, even bringing him presents of food. But as his sons grew older, they did not want to work as farmers, and they began to take whatever they needed from the local farms and villages. They carried off farmers' daughters to be their wives and give them sons, and so over the years the Doone family became bigger and bigger.

They began as robbers, but robbery had quickly led to violence and murder. The people of Exmoor were too afraid to fight back because the Doones were big, strong men and excellent fighters, and now only soldiers could hope to break into their valley and defeat them.

So there was no punishment for my father's murderer. We buried him quietly, and my mother was left without a husband, to manage our farm and take care of her three children. We were too young to be of much help to her yet. I was the oldest, then there was Annie, two years younger than me, then little Lizzie.

For a while, I wanted revenge. I was strong, and growing stronger every day. But my mother always calmed me down when I talked of revenge. She did not want to lose me too, and I used to worry about what would happen to her and my sisters if I were killed. We tried to get on with our lives, but we missed my father terribly. Sometimes my mother and Annie would remember him and cry, and sometimes John Fry saw me with tears in my eyes – which I said was because of the cold wind. Lizzie, though she was the cleverest of us all, was too young to really understand what had happened.

So the months passed. I learnt how to shoot with my father's gun, and I worked hard on the farm to help my mother.

—2—
A boy and a girl

Saint Valentine's Day, 1675, was the day that changed my life for ever, though I did not know it then.

I was fourteen. My mother had been ill and was not eating very well, so I went out to find something that she liked – good, fresh fish, caught from clear water.

I went first along the Lynn river that runs through our valley, then I turned into Bagworthy Water. Though I knew that this river led to Doone valley, I did not think about it. I went on catching fish and moving up the river, then suddenly found myself standing at the bottom of the cliffs outside Doone valley.

In front of me was a waterfall, a steep hill of smooth,

In front of me was a waterfall.

fast-moving water. It was a wild, lonely place, surrounded by tall trees, and it was already getting late. I knew I should turn for home – but I also wanted very much to see what was at the top of that waterfall. It looked a dangerous climb, but if I did not climb it, I would always remember that I was too frightened to do it.

So I climbed.

The water beat against my legs, once knocking me down so that I nearly drowned, but I pulled myself up and went on. When I reached the top at last, my arms and legs were aching and my feet were cut by the rocks. I fell in the grass, exhausted.

When I opened my eyes, for a few seconds I didn't know where I was. But, kneeling beside me, touching my face with a leaf, was a very young girl.

'Oh, I'm so glad,' she whispered softly, as I sat up and looked at her. 'Now you'll try to be better, won't you?'

I had never heard as sweet a sound as this girl's voice, nor seen anything as beautiful as the large dark eyes that watched me, full of care and wonder. I stared at her without speaking, noticing her long, shining black hair.

'What is your name?' she said, 'and how did you get here, and what have you got in your bag?'

'They're fish for my mother,' I said. 'Very special fish. But I'll give you some, if you like.'

'Dear me – you're so proud of them, when they're only fish! But look at your feet – they're bleeding. Let me tie something round them for you.'

'Oh, I'm not worried about them,' I said bravely. 'My name's John Ridd. What's your name?'

'Lorna Doone,' she answered, in a soft voice, and looked down at the grass. She seemed afraid of her own name. 'Lorna Doone. Didn't you know?'

I stood up and touched her hand, and tried to make her look at me, but she turned away. I felt sorry for her – and even more sorry when she started to cry.

'Don't cry,' I said. 'I'm sure you've never done any harm. I'll give you all my fish, Lorna, and catch some more for my mother.'

But she looked so sad, with the tears running down her face, that my heart ached for her and I gave her a kiss. At once my face turned red – here was I, just a simple farmer's boy, but she, though young, was clearly a lady and far above me.

She turned her head away, and I felt I should go. But I couldn't. She turned back to look at me.

'You must go,' she said. 'They will kill us if they find us together. You have found a way up into the valley, which they could never believe. You must go now, but when your feet are better, you can come and tell me how they are.' She smiled at me, and I could see that she liked me.

We talked for a while longer, but then a shout came down the valley. Lorna's face changed from playfulness to fear. We whispered our goodbyes, then Lorna ran away from me and lay in the grass, pretending to be asleep. I hid behind some rocks, and saw twelve cruel-looking men come walking down the valley, looking for Lorna. One of them – the biggest of them all, a man with a long black beard – found her. 'Here she is,' he said. 'Here's our little Queen.' He picked her up and kissed her so hard that I heard him. Then he put her on his shoulders, and carried her away. But as she went up the valley on the back of this frightening man, Lorna turned and secretly held up her hand to me.

Now I had to find a way out of the valley and get home. I almost broke my neck several times, climbing down the mountain, and I did not get home until long after dark. My mother was angry with me, but I would not say where I had been.

After my adventure, I thought a lot about the strange little girl I had met in Doone valley. But I never really imagined I would go back to the valley again. So after a while I thought less about her, and got on with my work on the farm.

—— 3 ——

Back to Doone valley

The months and the years went by, and I grew very tall and strong, as my father had been. By the time I had finished growing, I was bigger than any man on Exmoor, and could pick up John Fry with one hand and hold him in the air – until he begged me to put him down.

My sister Annie grew more and more beautiful every

year, with her wide blue eyes and soft brown hair. She was so kind and so gentle that everyone loved to be with her, and it is easy to understand why my mother's cousin, Tom Faggus, fell in love with her.

Tom Faggus was someone that our family was both proud and ashamed of. For a time he was one of the most famous robbers in England, and people still tell the stories of his adventures all over the country. He had been an honest farmer once, but a rich man had used the law to steal his farm, and after that Tom took his revenge on all rich men he met on the roads. Perhaps that was why he was so popular with the people, as he stole only from the rich, gave generously to the poor and the sick, and never hurt anyone in his life.

While I was still a boy, he came to our farm one day, asking my mother for food and a bed for the night. At first my mother told him to go away, fearing that we children would learn bad ways from him, but in the end she agreed.

'You may be a bad man in some ways,' she said to him, 'but there are far worse than you. So come and sit by the fire, and eat whatever we can give you.'

Tom always had a smile and a good word for everybody, and was great fun to be with. All the time he was with us, I saw Annie looking at him very kindly, and over the years we had many more visits from him.

As for Lizzie, I never thought anyone would fall in love with her! She was small and thin, and perhaps a little too clever – you never knew what she was going to say next.

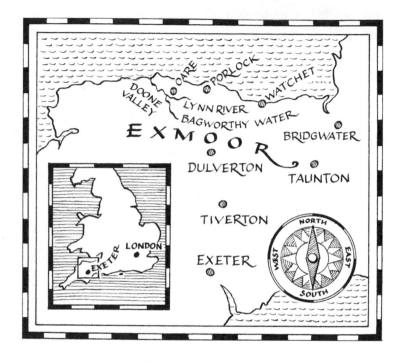

But I should not talk in this way about my own sister.

My mother didn't seem to grow any older, and was still pretty, and as good-hearted as ever. She had never forgotten my father, and as the years went by, she still sometimes cried for him.

In all this time, if I thought of Lorna Doone at all, it was only as a kind of dream. And the Doone men went on robbing and killing, just as they pleased.

Then one Christmas, when I was twenty-one, my Uncle Ben was robbed by the Doones on his way across Exmoor.

He had been coming to visit us, and when he didn't arrive, my mother sent me out to look for him. I found him on a high, lonely path, tied on to his horse with his nose to its tail. He was very angry, and wanted revenge on the Doones. He asked me to show him where they lived, so that he could learn the best way to attack them 'when the time was right'. So a day or two later I took him up into the mountains that looked down on the valley.

I had not been back this way since I was fourteen, and on the way, I thought of the girl I had met in this valley – of her lovely dark eyes, her sweet smile, her sadness . . . and her loneliness.

At the top of a steep cliff, we looked down into the long, green Doone valley. At either end was a narrow gap in the mountain walls. At the further end was the waterfall which I had climbed seven years before, and at the other was what we called the Doone-gate. This was two rocky cliffs facing each other, with only a narrow path between them. It was like the gate of a castle, and it seemed impossible to break into the valley. But Uncle Ben saw a way.

'Do you see how you could attack them?' he said. 'If you put big guns along the cliffs on both sides, and fired down into the valley, you could defeat the Doones in half an hour.'

But I was not listening to him. I was looking across to the waterfall end of the valley, and a little figure in white walking there, someone who walked with a very light step.

My heart began to beat more quickly, and the blood came to my face. In seven years I had half-forgotten her, and she would never remember me, I thought. But at that moment, once and for all, I saw my future in front of me: Lorna Doone.

On the way home I was quiet, and Uncle Ben asked me many times what was wrong with me. But I could not tell him. The truth was, I had decided to go back into Doone valley.

I waited until Saint Valentine's day – the exact day when I had first entered the valley. Again, I followed the river, and again I climbed the waterfall. Although I was seven years older, the climb was not easy. When I got to the top, I looked around me carefully.

In the early spring sunshine, the valley was beautiful. As I looked at the stream and the fields of grass on either side of it, I forgot about any dangers – and then I heard someone singing, in a beautiful voice. At first I hid behind a rock, but when I looked out, I saw the lovely sight of Lorna Doone coming towards me, along by the side of the stream. Her beauty frightened me. How could I – only a farmer – talk to her? But something seemed to pull at me and I came out from behind the rock.

At first, she turned to run away, not knowing who I was, but then I said, 'Lorna Doone!' and she seemed to remember me. A smile broke out on her face.

'I'm John Ridd,' I said, 'the boy who gave you those beautiful fish, seven years ago today.'

I saw Lorna Doone coming towards me,
along by the side of the stream.

'Oh, yes – the boy who was so frightened that he hid behind those rocks. I remember.'

'And do you remember how kind you were, and how you wanted to help me? And then you went away, riding on a big man's shoulders, and pretending you had never seen me. But you looked back and waved at me.'

15

'Oh, yes. I remember everything, because it isn't often I see anybody, except – I mean . . . Well, I just remember, that's all. But don't *you* remember, sir, how dangerous this place is?'

But I couldn't answer her. She had kept her eyes on me all the time – large eyes, of a softness and brightness and beauty that took my breath away. I felt love taking hold of me – a love too deep and too strong for words. How could I explain feelings that I did not really understand myself?

She turned her eyes away from me. 'I don't think you can possibly know, John Ridd, the dangers of this place, or what its people are like.'

I could see that she herself was very frightened. She was trembling, from fear that someone might see me while I was there, and hurt me. To tell the truth, I also grew afraid, and thought I had better go and say no more, until the next time I came.

I touched her white hand softly. 'Don't be afraid,' I said. 'I'll go now, but I'll come again soon, and bring you some fresh eggs from our farm.'

She reminded me again of the danger. 'But,' she went on, 'it seems that you still remember your secret way in,' and she smiled at me kindly.

4

Lorna's story

I went home with my head in the clouds, and my heart on fire with love. All that week I could not stop thinking about Lorna, and I did my work on the farm in a dream. Soon, I went to see her again.

This time when she saw me, she came quickly towards me. 'Mr Ridd, are you mad?' she said. 'There are men on guard all round the valley. We must hide at once.' She took my hand and led me to her secret place, which was a kind of room hidden in the rock of the mountain. It was a green, peaceful place, open to the sky above, but the only way into it was through a narrow entrance in a cave.

I gave her the eggs I had brought her as a present, and at this she began to cry.

'What have I done?' I asked.

'It's nothing you've done,' she said. 'It's just a sadness that I feel when I see anything from the world outside – and you've been very kind, and I'm not used to kindness.'

I wanted to put my arms around her, and kiss her, but I knew this would be wrong. So I sat and listened, and I think this made her like me more, because she began to tell me her life story. She told me everything – everything except what her feelings were towards John Ridd.

'Only two people ever listen to me, or try to help me,' she began. 'One is my grandfather, Sir Ensor Doone, and the other is my uncle, a clever man, whom they call the

Counsellor. My grandfather is a very old and very hard man – except with me. He seems to know what is right and wrong, but not to want to think about it. And the Counsellor smiles a lot and talks about what is right and good – but he never does a good thing himself.

'My Aunt Sabina used to take care of me, and she taught me very carefully. She was a good person, honest and kind, and when she died, it was like losing a mother. Now there is only one woman I can talk to – Gwenny, my servant. She is my closest friend.

'I don't remember my father, but they say he was the eldest son of Sir Ensor Doone, and the bravest and best of them all. They say, because of that, that I am their "Queen".

'I dream of a world outside this one, Mr Ridd – a world of peace. This valley is green and beautiful, but all around me is violence and robbery, and stupid behaviour. I can't come down to their level. I can't forget myself and live like them. And strange questions come to me, that they can never answer. When I try to think about the past, about my early childhood, I can't remember anything. I want to know what I am, and why I am in this place. I suppose you think that's strange. Perhaps people who are happy and at peace don't need to ask questions like those.'

Here, Lorna began to cry again. I could think of nothing to say, but I dried her eyes for her.

'Mr Ridd, I am ashamed and angry at myself for talking so much, like this. But you, who have a mother who loves you, and sisters, and a quiet home, can't tell how lonely it is to live as I do.

'I have this secret place to come to, because I begged them for it. Only grandfather and the Counsellor come here – and sometimes Carver, the Counsellor's son. No one in the valley is as strong or brave as him. But he is not like his father. He is rough and violent, always quick to be angry, and will listen to no opinion except his own. There is talk of him wanting to marry me, but I would rather die than marry Carver Doone.

'Now you see how unhappy I am here. I would escape, and go anywhere, but I know it would hurt my grandfather.'

This was too much for Lorna, and she couldn't tell me

'I have this secret place to come to.'

any more. She broke down and cried. I talked to her gently and kindly until she began to worry again about the danger I was in. I said I would come back and see her again, but she made me promise not to come back for another month – so that I would not add to her problems with fears about me. During that time, we agreed that if she were in any danger, she would put a dark coat over a white rock, near her secret room. I would be able to see this from a hill above the valley, and then I would come.

—— 5 ——

To London

But I was not able to see Lorna again as soon as I had hoped. Before the month had passed, I was called away from home, in a very strange and unexpected way.

One afternoon, as I was outside the house feeding the horses, a stranger rode up to our gate and shouted at me. He was a tough-looking, hard-faced man, about forty years old, with small, quick eyes, and he was dressed very differently from the way we dress in Exmoor. He said he was looking for Plover's Barrows farm, and a man called John Ridd. When I told him he had found them both, he introduced himself as Jeremy Stickles, a servant of the King, and he gave me a letter. I looked at him in alarm, but he said there was nothing in the letter to worry me.

At the top of the letter, my name was written in large letters. I read:

To JOHN RIDD:

This letter is to order you to appear before the King's judges in London, and tell them anything you know about some matters which may be harmful to the King and the country.

Jeremy Stickles seemed very pleased by my fear and surprise at the letter, but he said again that no one was going to hurt me. All I had to do was tell the truth.

When my mother read the letter, she became very worried and began to cry. She wondered how the King had heard of me, and what he wanted to do with me. But Mr Stickles, who wasn't really as hard as he seemed, explained everything carefully to her. He told her that the King only knew of me because the stories of my great size and strength had reached even London. He had heard I was a good man, and thought I could help him, that was all.

This made my mother feel better, but I was very unhappy. I was thinking of Lorna. How could I tell her I was going away? I had promised not to go back to the valley for a month, and that was still a few days away. But how terrible it would be if she came to look for me at the end of the month, and I was not there! I would have to break my promise and go before the agreed time.

Mr Stickles was happy to stay at the farm for one or two days, to try our good Exmoor food. So I used the time to look for Lorna. But I saw nothing of her in the valley, and no signal that she needed me. There was nothing else

I could do. Mr Stickles wanted to go, and I had to leave for London without seeing her.

––––– •●• –––––

A journey to London was both long and dangerous in those days, because of all the robbers on the roads. As I said goodbye to my mother and sisters and took my last look at the farmhouse, I felt very miserable. But Jeremy Stickles was a good companion. As we rode, he told me many amusing stories of London life, and we became the best of friends.

I did not like London. It was a crowded, dirty place, not at all like Exmoor – and, even worse, I had to wait more than two months before the King's judges were ready to see me. There was a lot of trouble in London at that time, with arguments between the King and the City of London. Nobody had time to talk to John Ridd, but I was not allowed to leave and go home. At last, I was called to see Judge Jeffreys.

Jeremy Stickles had told me about Judge Jeffreys. He was the King's chief judge, and there were terrible stories about him. He became very angry if anyone argued with him, and he had sent many of the King's enemies to their deaths.

In the room I walked into, there were three men sitting on high seats, and they were dressed in very rich clothes. In front of each of them was a desk, with pen and paper. The man in the middle seemed to be the most important. He was a big, heavy man, with a square chin and a kind of fire in his eyes. He was a man that almost anyone would be afraid of. This was certainly Judge Jeffreys.

He gave me a terrible stare, and asked me who I was and where I came from. When I had told him, he said: 'Well done, John Ridd. You have answered me without fear. I remember this matter now. I will ask you some questions.' He looked at me more closely. 'In Exmoor,' he said, 'there is a family of robbers. Is that true?'

I told him it was.

'And why isn't your local judge doing anything about them?'

Judge Jeffreys gave me a terrible stare.

23

'I suppose he's afraid, my Lord. The robbers are very strong, and their valley is hard to attack.'

'But they must still answer to the law!' Judge Jeffreys said. 'What's the name of these people, and how many of them are there?'

'They are the Doones, and we think there are about forty men in the valley.'

'I will do something about these thieves,' he said. 'Perhaps I will come down to the west myself.' But then he stared hard at me again, and asked: 'Is there any sign, in Exmoor, of any dislike of the King?'

'No, my Lord. We don't know much about him.'

'That's a good answer,' he laughed. 'But the King knows he has enemies in the country. I see you know nothing about them, though. You're a good man, John Ridd. Keep out of trouble. Keep away from the King's enemies, and from the Doones as well, and you will be safe. I was going to use you as a spy, but I see you're too honest. I will send someone else. But never tell anyone what I've said to you.' Here he stared at me very angrily, but when he saw he had frightened me enough, he smiled again. 'Now go home, John. I will remember you – and I don't think you will forget me.'

I had no money left to hire a horse for the journey back to Exmoor, so I had to walk the whole way. It took me seven days, and I was very glad to get home again.

6

Lorna's new troubles

When I arrived at the farm, Mother held me tightly and cried for half an hour. I gave everyone all the presents I had bought for them in London, but of course what I wanted to do most of all was find Lorna, and see how she was. I wanted to tell Mother all about her, but the thought of my father's murder by the Doones stopped me. There was little chance that Lorna would love me, so why should I worry my mother about it?

As soon as I could, I went to Doone valley – but, there, I could not believe my bad luck. When I looked from the cliff top, I saw Lorna's sign – her coat on a white rock! She had needed me, and now perhaps I was too late to help her.

I climbed round the outer cliffs to the waterfall, and was soon looking down towards the green fields of the valley. I stood and waited – not caring, now, if anyone saw me – and then at last a little figure came towards me.

I could see she was frightened, so I went towards her slowly.

'Miss Lorna, I saw your sign on the white rock, that you needed me.'

'Oh, yes, but that was a long time ago – two months or more, sir,' and she looked away. She looked so sad that I thought everything was over between us, and tried to turn away and go. But when she saw that I was hurt and ashamed, she ran towards me and took my hands.

'Oh John, I'm sorry. I didn't mean to hurt you,' she said. How happy I was, to hear her call me 'John'! Then she led me away to her secret room, through the cave in the mountain. Since it was partly open to the sky, plants and flowers were able to grow there, and now, in the late summer, it was beautiful.

She could not look at me at first, but when she did, I could see that she had been crying.

'My grandfather is not well,' she said. 'And now Carver Doone and his evil father, the Counsellor, have more control over the Doones. They want me to marry Carver. Not immediately – I am only seventeen. But they want me to give my promise, in front of my grandfather, that I will marry Carver. They say it's for the peace of the Doones. That's why I left the signal out for you, Mr Ridd. They wanted to force me, but my grandfather would not let them. They won't do it – at least while grandfather is alive. But they're watching me, and following me, and I can't go where I want any more. Gwenny is helping me. If she wasn't, I couldn't even be here, talking to you. But perhaps even you don't care about me any more.'

Her eyes filled with tears, and I quickly explained about my journey to London. I told her how much I had missed her and how I had worried about her all this time. Then I showed her the present I had brought her from London – a ring with blue and white stones. At first she cried even more, and then came and sat so close to me that I began to

I put the ring on her finger.

tremble. Then I picked up her hand and, while I was
pretending to look at its beauty and softness, put the ring
on her finger.

'Oh, Mr Ridd!' she said, her face going red. 'I thought
you were much too honest and simple ever to do something
like this! No wonder you are good at catching fish. But
no, John, you have not caught me yet, not completely,
though I like you very much – and if you will only keep
away, out of danger, I will like you even more.'

With tears still in her eyes, which seemed to come partly
from wanting to love me as much as I loved her, she kissed
my head. Then she gently took my ring off her finger, and,

kissing it three times, gave it back to me. 'John, I cannot take it now,' she said. 'It would not be right. I will try to love you dearly – as dearly as you could wish. Keep the ring for me until then. Something tells me I will earn it – very soon.'

This time, I promised Lorna that I would not come back to see her for two months. If Carver or the Counsellor became violent towards her, she would signal me as before. Two months was a long time to wait, but because of what she had said to me, I was happy.

Very soon after that I told my sister Annie about Lorna. I knew she would keep my secret, and it was good to be able to talk to her about my troubles. Then she gave me a surprise. Tom Faggus had asked her to marry him, and she had agreed. But although Mother liked Tom, we both knew she would not like her daughter to marry him! And how would she feel about me wanting to marry Lorna Doone? We promised to help each other, if we could.

———— •●• ————

On the very first day after the agreed two months, I went to find Lorna. But this time when I got to the top of the waterfall, she was not there.

I waited for hours, but she didn't come. Then I saw something that made me afraid for her. While I was hiding behind a tree, a big man appeared, walking lazily down the valley. He wore a wide hat, a dark jacket and tall boots, and he carried a gun over his shoulder. As he came closer, I could see his face clearly, and there was something in it that turned me cold, with a kind of horror. It was a face that never smiled – and in his eyes was only cruelty. I did not doubt that this was Carver Doone.

And this was the man, I thought angrily, who planned to marry Lorna. He had no idea I was there, but I almost hoped he would discover me. If we could fight hand to hand, a fight between us would be fair, as he was the only man I knew who was near my size. But I knew it would be a mistake to fight Carver. Whether I won or lost, the Doones would learn about me, and I would never see Lorna again.

When, by the evening, Lorna had still not appeared, I went home. I went back to the valley every day for two weeks, but never saw Lorna. I saw Carver Doone again, though, walking with his gun round the top of the valley, and that worried me. I was sure that Lorna was in danger; I would go into Doone valley and find her.

This time, I decided to go by the Doone-gate. It was a dangerous route, but I knew it would be useful to know how the Doones defended the main entrance to their valley.

At night the Doone-gate, with its tall black cliffs and sharp rocks, was a frightening place. There were no guards outside, and very quietly and carefully, I entered the narrow, dark path between the cliffs. Soon I saw a light shining round a corner of the cliff and, staying close to the rock wall, I stepped carefully up to the corner and looked round it.

Two guards were sitting by the light, with their guns on

the ground beside them. Here, the cliffs widened out into broken, rocky ground, with deep shadows between the rocks. The guards were clearly not expecting an attack, and were drinking and talking. I stood and watched, and while I was wondering what to do, they began to argue, and then to fight. This gave me my chance. I went slowly along the cliff wall, and then moved quickly into the shadows of the open rocky ground. The guards were so busy with their fight that they did not see or hear me, and I was soon past them and going down the hillside into Doone valley.

Lorna had told me that her grandfather's house was the first one after the gate. So, carefully and quietly, I went towards it and stood below one of the windows. I could not shout or call out because there were other guards around the small village, but luck was with me that night. Lorna came to the window, opened it, and looked out up at the night sky. I whispered her name. She jumped in alarm, but then looked down and saw who I was.

'John!' she said. 'Oh, John, you must be mad!'

'I was going mad, because I didn't know what had happened to you. But you knew I would come.'

'I hoped you would! But do you see they have put these bars across my window?' She put her hand out through them, and I took it and kissed it, and then held both her hands in mine.

'Oh, John, you'll make me cry,' she said, though I could see she had already been crying. 'We can never be together.

Why should I make you unhappy? Try to forget me.'

'Never,' I said. 'If we want to belong to one another, Lorna, no one can stop us – only God, if he wishes it. Now tell me, why have you been kept in prison here?'

'My grandfather is very ill now. I am afraid he won't live long. The Counsellor and his son are the masters of the valley. They want me here where they can see me, so that I can't escape from Carver; and Gwenny is not allowed to move about now, so I couldn't send you a message, or signal you. You must watch this house day and night, John, if you wish to save me. There is nothing they wouldn't do, if my poor grandfather – Oh, I can't think only of myself, when I should think of him.'

'How can I leave you even one more night here, Lorna?' I said.

'You must, John,' she said. 'You're so brave, but I love you too much to let you stay any longer. Yes, it's true! But I cannot leave my grandfather while he is dying. So, if you love me, John, you must go.'

'I'll go for now. But when I hear that your grandfather has died, I will come and get you out of here. If I promise to take you safely away, will you come with me?'

'Yes,' she said. 'Of course I will.'

So now I took her hand in mine again, and put my ring on her finger. I had kept it in my pocket since the day I had first brought it to her. This time she kept it, though she cried and held my hand tightly.

'Oh, John. This can never, never be!' she said.

7

Lorna leaves the valley

I left Doone valley by my own secret route and went home
to make plans for bringing Lorna to the farm. It was time
to tell Mother all about Lorna and the danger she was in.

At first Mother was very angry and unhappy at my news.
She talked wildly about going away and leaving the farm,
but after a time she began to calm down.

'When you see her, Mother,' I said, 'I'm sure you will
love her like a daughter. And I know she will love you
with all her heart – she is so good and gentle.'

Mother was too kind-hearted to be angry for long. She
cried a little more, then smiled and said, 'Well, God knows
what is good for us. You must bring her here, John, and I
will teach her how to be a farmer's wife.'

Lorna and I had agreed a new signal. There was a tall
tree near her grandfather's house, which I could see from
the cliff top above the valley. In the top branches of the
tree there were seven large birds' nests from the last
summer. Gwenny could climb like a cat, and if one morning
I saw only six nests, then Lorna's grandfather was dead
and she was in great danger.

It was a bad winter that year. We had more snow than
anyone could remember, and on Exmoor the snow was
soon so deep that no one could walk on it safely. I had to
find a way to cross this, but I had an idea. Lizzie had once
shown me a book about the icy countries of the far north,

32

where people wore 'snow shoes'. The book had pictures of these wide, flat shoes which stopped travellers' feet going down through the snow. For the first time I thanked my sister in my heart for reading so many books! I found some wood and animal skins, and soon I had made some snow shoes, like the ones in Lizzie's book.

We had a sled on the farm, which we used when the ground was covered in ice. A horse could not pull it in this weather – but, with my snow shoes, I could! I could use it to carry Lorna and her servant.

Some days later I saw only six birds' nests in the tree, and that evening I tied myself to the sled, and left for Doone valley. I took the sled to the waterfall, which was now a fall of ice, and tied it up there. Then I continued on foot, going around the south side of the valley towards the Doone-gate. But when I looked down, I saw there was a quicker way to reach Lorna. The sides of the valley, like

In the top branches there were seven large birds' nests.

everything else, were covered in deep snow, and here the snow was smooth and icy. I looked around to check that there were no Doones in sight, then sat down on the icy snow and pushed myself off. In seconds I had slid all the way down the mountainside, and landed in a hill of soft snow at the bottom.

At Sir Ensor's house, I whispered Lorna's name below the window, as before. This time, Gwenny let me in, when she was sure who I was. But inside I saw a terrible sight. Gwenny looked almost mad with hunger, and Lorna lay back on a chair, as white as the valley all around us.

'Good God!' I said, and ran to her. I took her in my arms but she was so weak that she could not speak at first.

'We've been kept in here for days without food,' said Gwenny. 'And they were going to keep us here until Lorna agreed to marry Carver.'

'We must leave at once,' I said. 'Will you come with me, Lorna? I promise to take you safely through the snow.'

Lorna gave me her lovely smile. 'Of course I will, dear,' she whispered. 'Of course I will.'

'And you too, of course, Gwenny,' I said. 'Be quick now, and help me to get your mistress ready.'

From outside, I had heard the sounds of singing. There were usually guards around the house, Gwenny told me, but tonight the Doones were drinking and dancing to welcome Carver as their new leader. This would give us our chance – with all this happening, the robbers would never notice us leaving.

We were soon ready. I picked up my beautiful Lorna and carried her through the snow and the darkness to the other end of the valley. Gwenny was able to follow us, putting her feet in the places where my snow shoes had been. I made Lorna comfortable in the sled, with her little servant beside her, and I told her to hold on to Lorna tightly. The waterfall was now a path of ice – very steep

I made Lorna comfortable in the sled.

and dangerous, but I was able to take the sled down it, using my stick, and all my strength, to stop it going too fast on the ice.

When we were down the waterfall, I tied myself to the sled and began to pull. It was hard work for me – but the best work I had ever done in my life! There was no time to lose, with Lorna so weak from hunger and cold, so I pulled fast, and an hour later we were home.

My mother and sisters came to the door, and helped me to carry Lorna in. We put her in a chair by the fire, and gave her some soup. Then she slept, while I watched over her. After a time, she began to wake up. She put her trembling hands into mine, and looked at me with so much love in her eyes that I could not find the words to speak to her. We sat like this for several minutes, and then we heard a little sound behind us.

It was Mother, crying with happiness to see us so loving. At this, Lorna got up and went to her. She knelt beside Mother's chair and looked up into her face. Mother put her hand on Lorna's hair. 'My sweet child,' she said softly.

A few days later, when Lorna and I were sitting together by the fire, she said to me:

'John, you gave me a beautiful ring, and now I want to give you something. It is only a very poor, old thing, but it's all I have. My grandfather gave it to me before he died. I hope you will take it.'

Then she put on my finger the strangest ring I had ever seen. It was very old, and there was a picture on it. It was hard to see what the picture was, but it looked almost like a cat in a tree.

'I shall wear it, my love,' I said, 'until the day I die.'

—— 8 ——

The attack

Soon everybody in our part of Exmoor knew that Lorna Doone was at Plover's Barrows farm. So I knew the Doones would come looking for Lorna as soon as they could. But, for now, the weather saved us. They could not move in the snow, and when the rains came in spring, they had even bigger problems. The rains were heavy, and when the snow also turned to water, the rivers became very high. In Doone valley the robbers' homes were almost under water. They needed most of their men to take care of their village. If they attacked us, we knew it could not be with as many men as they would like.

Spring also brought a visitor for Annie. The snows had kept Tom Faggus away from the farm all winter, but now he came to see her, and he had something to tell her.

'Before the snows came,' he said, 'I went to London. And I have something to show for it.' Then out of his pocket, he took a letter. It looked very important, and had the King's sign on it. 'What do you think it is?'

We all looked at it, but it was full of long lawyers' words and no one could understand what it meant.

'I'll tell you what it means,' laughed Tom. 'It means

that I am not a criminal any more. This letter says that the King is ready to forget all my years as a robber, and I am a free man.'

We all wondered how this could be, but then Tom explained. 'I spoke to Judge Jeffreys. He knows me. He said, "If you promise never to rob again, you can go free. There's enough for the King to worry about in this country already, with all his enemies. So if we can forget about you, that's good enough for us."'

Everyone felt proud of Tom. We thought it had been very brave of him to go to Judge Jeffreys. But now he had something even better to tell us. With the money he still had, Tom had bought some land. He was going to live an honest life, and be a farmer again.

So we were not surprised when Tom asked Mother if he could marry Annie. Mother was not very sure of the new 'farmer Faggus'. She was afraid that he would get bored with farming and go back to being a robber. But she could see that he loved Annie very much, and between us, Annie and I managed to persuade her.

———— •●• ————

Now we began to prepare for the Doones' attack. Though the rivers were still high, people had begun to see a few of the robbers out on the roads, and we knew it would not be long before we would have to fight them.

As we were preparing, we received another visitor: my old friend Jeremy Stickles. This time, though, he had not been sent to find me. To our surprise, he told us that he had been spying in Exmoor for many months. He had been sent down this way again by Judge Jeffreys and the King.

'You must not tell anyone what I'm doing,' he said. 'But I have been sent to do important work. The King has many enemies, and now I have been given some soldiers – though only a few – to help me look for them. But I have to ask you: can my soldiers and I stay here for a while?'

I agreed immediately. When the Doones attacked, it would be a great help to have soldiers staying in the house. I told Jeremy all about Lorna, and he promised to help defend our farmhouse against any Doone attack.

The next day Stickles came with his men. There were only six of them, but even to have these was a help. All we could do now was wait, and be ready each night for an attack.

One day I came home late from the fields, and found all the women trembling with fear. Lorna had seen Carver Doone!

She had gone out in the evening to look at some flowers by our stream. There were thick bushes on the other side, and when Lorna looked up, she saw two cruel black eyes staring at her. She was too frightened to move. Carver could not cross the stream because the water was too high, but he lifted his gun and fired at the ground by Lorna's feet.

'Unless you come back tomorrow,' he said, 'and tell me how to destroy that farmer, Ridd, who will soon be a dead

man because of you, this will be the place of your death.'

Lorna told us this, trembling. We knew that Carver would not wait until tomorrow, and we got ready for an attack that night.

When the Doones attacked a farm, they always started fires in the hay ricks first – to frighten everyone and show what they could do. So when darkness came, I went with my best gun and a heavy stick to one of the hay ricks, and waited beside it.

I had made sure that Lorna stayed in the house, but little Gwenny climbed a tree near the river. From there she could see up the river to the only place where it was possible to cross. Soon the moon came up, and before very long,

'Kill every man and every child, and burn the farm.'

Gwenny came running towards me.

'Ten of them, coming across the river,' she said. 'They'll be here in a minute.'

'Go into the house and tell Mr Stickles and his men. I'll stay here and watch,' I said.

The robbers broke down our gate, and rode towards the house. I could see the soldiers hiding in the shadows, waiting for the order to fire, but the Doones then turned towards the hay ricks.

'Kill every man and every child, and burn the farm,' came the deep voice of Carver Doone. 'Start over there.' He was pointing to the hay rick where I was, though he could not see me. 'But remember, Lorna is mine, and I

41

will kill any man who touches her.'

As Carver spoke, I pointed my gun at him, but – will you believe me? – I didn't shoot. I had never killed a man, nor even badly hurt one. I did not think it was an easy thing to do. Now, I can say that I wish I had killed him. But I put my gun down, and picked up my stick – a more honest weapon than a gun, I thought.

Two young Doones came towards me, with burning sticks. The first put his stick to the hay rick I was standing near, and it started to burn. I hit him on the arm, and heard his bone break as he fell over with a shout of pain. The other man ran to see what had happened, and I took his fire stick and broke it. Then he jumped at me, but I caught him, broke his arm, and threw him on top of his friend.

I could still see Carver and wanted to jump at him – but I knew he would simply shoot me. While I was thinking about it, there came a loud noise and six tongues of flame from near the farmhouse. Stickles had ordered his men to fire at the Doones as they came towards the house. Two fell and the others ran back. They had something to think about now; no one had ever fought the Doones as we were doing that night.

Now my moment had come. I came out from my place near the burning rick. I knew Carver Doone by his size even in the shadowy moonlight, and I took hold of him by the beard. 'Do you call yourself a man?' I said.

For a second he was too surprised to do anything. No

one had ever looked at him the way I did now. He lifted his gun, but I was too quick for him and knocked it out of his hand.

'Now, Carver Doone, take warning,' I said. 'You think you are so much better than everyone else, but you are no more than an evil robber. Lie low in the dirt from which you came.'

Then I kicked his feet from under him and knocked him down. When they saw that he was down, the other Doones ran, but Carver simply got up and walked away, shouting at me and everyone.

We wondered whether to chase the Doones, but Mr Stickles said it would be too dangerous on the moor in the dark. One thing was certain: the robbers had known defeat that night on our farm – something they had never experienced since the day they came to Exmoor. And they went home without four of their men. Two were dead, shot by the soldiers, and the other two were the men whose arms I had broken by the hay ricks. We buried the dead men in the fields, and Jeremy Stickles sent the two wounded men to the prison in Taunton.

— 9 —

Lorna's true story

The Doones' attack had been defeated. We knew that they would come again, as soon as they could, in larger numbers. But for now, Jeremy Stickles gave me something else to think about. My dearest wish was to marry Lorna as soon as I could, but after Jeremy's story I began to wonder if it would ever be possible.

A few days after our battle with the Doones, Jeremy said he had something to say to me.

'John, I didn't think the time was right to tell you this before. But now you must hear what I have to say. As you know, I've been riding around Exmoor for many months, looking for information that might be useful to the King. I remembered all that you told me about Lorna, and I think I have discovered something about her. It may not be easy for you to hear, John. Are you ready?'

'I will do my best,' I said.

So he began his story.

'Six or seven months ago, before the snows began, I stopped at an inn on my way from Dulverton to Watchet. The inn was all by itself, right by the sea, and was very quiet. I was the only person staying there, and the woman who owned the inn sat down and talked to me during my meal. She was dark and foreign-looking, and intelligent. I was very interested to know how an unusual woman like her had come to live in this lonely inn, and she told me her story.

'She said that she was from Italy, and her name was Benita. Many years ago, while she was working in Rome, she had met an English family. They were travelling in Italy because they'd had a terrible argument in England with another family. Benita did not know much about the argument, except that it had been about land.

'Benita liked this English family. They were very rich, but they were also kind. So when they asked her to travel with them and take care of their children, she agreed. She loved the children – a little girl and boy – so she was very happy in her work.

'At first everything went well. Together, Benita and the family travelled up through northern Italy and into France. But on the French side of the Pyrenees, the husband of the family had a riding accident and was killed.

'His wife was deeply unhappy, and would not move from the place where he had died for many months. But finally she decided to go home to England and try to start life again. Benita stayed with her, and they took a ship to the Devon coast. They stayed at Exeter, and then left in a coach for Watchet, in the north of Somerset. The lady had a house there, where she planned to live.

'They were warned, at Dulverton, about robbers on the roads, but the lady would not listen. She even travelled at night, which, as we know, is a very dangerous thing to do. So of course they were attacked by robbers. It happened near the sea. The coachmen drove onto the sand, and the robbers followed on their horses. The coach's wheels began to go down in the soft sand, and as the robbers came nearer, the lady pointed to one of them and said: "I know that man! He is our family's old enemy."

'Then a great wave crashed against the coach and turned it over. Benita hit her head on the door and could not

'Benita saw her mistress sitting on a rock.'

remember what happened. The next thing she knew was
that she was lying on the sand and the robbers had gone.
She looked around for her mistress and saw her sitting on
a rock, with her dead son in her arms. The little girl had
disappeared. Benita and the two coachmen took the lady
into the town, but later that night, she died. This is a sad
story!' said Jeremy. 'Give me a drink, boy!'

I saw that there were tears in the brave man's eyes.

'What was the lady's name?' I asked. 'And what
happened to the little girl? And why did Benita stay there?'

'I will answer the last question first,' said Jeremy. 'That's
the easiest. Benita stayed in that place because the Doones

– if that's who they were – stole everything from the coach, and she had no money. She could not go back to Italy. She married a man who lived near the place because he was kind and could give her a home.'

'But the little girl, Jeremy. What happened to her?'

'John – can't you see it? You are more likely to know than anyone in the world! As certain as I sit here, that little girl is Lorna Doone!'

The truth was, I had guessed this, almost from the beginning of Jeremy's story. But it was almost too painful to believe, and I wanted Jeremy to say it. When he described the coach leaving Dulverton, the picture was very clear to me – because I remembered that coach, with the foreign-looking woman, the beautiful lady, the little boy, and the young dark-haired girl. I had seen them – on the day John Fry came to collect me from school, on the day I learnt my father had died.

I also remembered the frightening sight I saw later that night: of the Doones riding with the things they had stolen, and the one with a little girl across his horse in front of him. I also remembered my anger. Now I saw how the very same day had been the blackest and unhappiest of both my and Lorna's childhood days, and how from the very start, our lives had been joined together.

But there was still one question to answer. 'What was the family's name?' I said.

'The father was Lord Dugal – he came from a very grand family. But there is more to this. Look at your ring, John –

the one that Lorna gave you. Look at that strange sign, of a cat in a tree. I saw that same sign above the inn door! That is the sign of the House of Lorne. It is the family that Lorna's mother came from. John, your Lorna belongs to one of the richest and most famous families in England!'

—— 10 ——
Gone

Now I had to tell Lorna. So, a day or two later, with an aching heart, I went to tell her what Jeremy had said. I'm afraid that some of my sadness was for me, because now, more than ever, it was certain: Lorna was far, far above me. How could she possibly marry a simple farmer now?

We sat in the garden, and she held my hand while she listened without a word to what I said. But by the look in her beautiful eyes, and by her trembling hand, I could tell how she was feeling. At the end, she turned away and cried for her poor parents. But she spoke not even one word of anger about what had happened to them.

Then, to my surprise, she turned to me and caught me in her arms and kissed me as she had never done before. 'John, I have you. You, and only you. And I want no one else. It does not matter how rich or important my family is.'

It was impossible to doubt those clear deep eyes, and bright trembling lips. But I was afraid of what the future would bring. To me, she was Lorna Doone, but to the world, she was Lady Lorna Dugal – young, beautiful, and rich. And if the world learnt about her, it would want to take her away from me.

———— •●• ————

Now the date of Tom and Annie's wedding was decided, and I went to Dulverton to buy a present for them. As I was riding, I had time to think more about what Jeremy had told me.

It was clear from his story that Lorna's mother's family, the Lornes, were the family with whom Sir Ensor Doone had argued about land, before he came to Exmoor. This explained why Lorna's mother had called him her 'old enemy', when she saw him that terrible night. And this must be why the Doones had carried Lorna away and kept her, and never told her who she really was. If they could marry her to a Doone before she learnt the truth, perhaps they hoped in this way to get the Lorne family's land. They would be rich and important again – and at the same time have revenge on the Lornes. But it would have to be a lawful marriage, so Sir Ensor had taken good care of Lorna and kept her safe from the wild Doone men. And Carver, seeing how beautiful Lorna had become, had decided to marry her himself.

In Dulverton I stayed with Uncle Ben, and his granddaughter, Ruth. She was a beautiful and intelligent girl, and had often been very kind to me.

I did not spend too much money on a present in Dulverton. I was saving for my own wedding to Lorna. I had told her that if her family's great riches ever came to her, I would not touch any of her money. In fact, we had both agreed that we would give nearly everything to the poor, and live simply.

Three days later, dreaming hopefully of the future, I walked into the kitchen at home – and saw immediately that something was wrong. Then Mother and Annie told me that Lorna had gone.

Two men had come from London. They were lawyers and had been sent by the King's judges to take Lorna away. The judges had heard that she was still alive, and they and her uncle had ordered her to come to London. Her uncle was Earl Brandir – the last living person in her family – and Lorna now had to live with him. She could not refuse. She was not yet twenty-one, so she had to do what this uncle and the judges said. Of course, she had begged the lawyers not to take her. But they said they had their orders, and they could not wait for her to say goodbye to me.

Upstairs, by my bed, Lorna had left me a letter. I ran up to read it. She said she loved me, and she said 'Goodbye', and the letter finished like this:

John, we have been through so many troubles and dangers, but there is no doubt that we belong together. You must believe me. Whatever happens, I am yours.

But I could not stop myself from thinking: 'It is over.'

———— •●• ————

Later, I wondered how the judges and Lorna's uncle had heard that Lorna was still alive. Perhaps Jeremy Stickles

I saw immediately that something was wrong.

had mentioned her in his spying reports to the King and Judge Jeffreys. Perhaps the Doones themselves had sent the news to London – in order to get their revenge on me. The daughter of so famous a family would not be allowed to marry a simple farmer and live quietly in Devon. Jeremy was away on one of his spying trips now, so I could not ask him about it. But, anyway, there was nothing he could do.

The weeks and months passed, and life on the farm seemed lonely and empty. After Annie married Tom, and went to live with him, I felt even more alone. Sometimes I used to go over and see her in her new home, but it was not the same as having her by my side, the friend and companion from my childhood days.

——11——
Tom Faggus in danger

We still lived in fear of another attack from the Doones, and now that the soldiers had gone we had no one to help us. The main reason for their first attack – Lorna – was gone, but I was sure that Carver now hated me with all his heart, and would destroy us all if he could.

However, Jeremy Stickles brought us some good news one day. The King had at last agreed that the robbers should be punished, and that Jeremy should do whatever was necessary to catch them. So perhaps the Doones were saving their strength, preparing for a much bigger fight than their argument with me.

Then something happened which made everyone afraid for the future. Suddenly, King Charles the Second died. There was terrible trouble in England, as everyone argued over who should be the new King, and soon fighting began.

I wondered if all this would bring any danger for Lorna. But the truth was, I knew very little about her now. She had not written to me since the day she had left, or even sent a message. I only knew what I had heard from travellers in the town. They said that young Lady Lorna Dugal was much talked about in London, as one of the most beautiful women in the city. I became more and more certain that she had forgotten all about John Ridd, among the brighter stars of London.

In June, the fighting became more serious. There was

now a new King – James, the son of Charles the Second – but many people in Dorset and Somerset were against him, and had joined an army of rebels. There was no chance now that Jeremy Stickles and his soldiers would fight the Doones. King James needed all his men to fight the rebels. At first we were very worried. Surely the Doones would attack us now. But the Doones had seen a new hope for their future. They had joined the King's enemies, hoping to win back their old land in the fighting. So they had sent most of their men to join the rebels, and were too busy again to worry about the Ridds – at least for a while.

As for me, I had decided that this battle between the King and his enemies was not my fight. Most people in the towns and villages around Oare were on the King's side and we gave no help to his enemies, but sensible people stayed at home. Too many men would die in the fighting anyway, without our joining them.

However, I did get involved in the troubles, because one rainy day Annie came to see us, with some bad news. She ran into the kitchen, her face wet with tears.

'Oh, John!' she cried. 'You must help me!'

'Whatever is the matter, Annie dear?' I said.

'It's Tom,' Annie cried. 'He's gone to join the rebels, and you must, oh, you must go after him and bring him back.'

We had been afraid of this. Tom could not forget the excitement of his old life and had become bored with farming. Mother was very unhappy and did not want me to go, but I had to help my unhappy sister. And although I knew it would be dangerous, I was quite glad of the chance of adventure. Perhaps – who knows? – I would learn some news of Lorna on my travels.

So I promised to fetch Annie's husband home, and early the next morning I rode away on our fastest horse. I went from town to town, asking for news of the fighting, but it was four days before I finally found the two armies at Bridgwater. There had been a great battle the night before, which the rebels had lost, and many of them now lay dead or dying on the battlefield. I shall never forget that terrible sight. I thought Tom must be dead, and I walked all over the battlefield, looking for his body. Several times I stopped in my search, to give some poor dying man a last drink from my water bottle.

After a time I found myself near an old farm building, and I suddenly saw that the riderless horse standing in the doorway was without doubt Tom Faggus's horse. I hurried into the building, and found Tom lying on the ground, badly wounded. He could still speak, but only in a whisper, because of the pain.

'Put me on my horse, John,' he said, 'and she'll take me home. No one can catch her – she's the fastest horse alive. It's my best chance of escaping.'

He was right. The King's soldiers were still riding around the battlefield, looking for rebels to kill. So I tied up Tom's wound as best I could, put him on his horse, and turned the horse's head for home.

'Thank you, John. I am safe now,' he whispered. He lay along his horse's neck, to close the wound in his side. 'But look out for yourself, John Ridd.'

I watched Tom's horse disappear into the distance, and only a minute later I turned and saw soldiers coming towards me. 'Stop,' they said, 'in the name of the King.'

'I'm not a rebel,' I said. 'I'm on the King's side and—'

But they would not listen to me. 'You are an enemy of the King,' they said, 'and the punishment is death.'

I tried to argue with them, and as they laid their hands on me, I knocked one soldier to the ground. This made them even angrier, and the captain ordered his men to tie me to a tree and shoot me at once.

There was nothing I could do against twenty men, so I

I knocked one soldier to the ground.

55

closed my eyes and tried to think about Lorna and my mother. The captain gave the order to fire, but at the same moment I heard a horse coming towards us, and another voice shouting, 'Stop!'

It was Jeremy Stickles! He rode his horse between me and the guns, and started to argue with the captain. His voice was the sweetest sound I had heard for a long time!

The argument was soon over. I heard Jeremy mention Judge Jeffreys once or twice, and before long he had persuaded the captain not to shoot me. 'This man, John Ridd, is my prisoner,' said Jeremy, 'and I shall take him to London for trial there.'

As we rode away together, I thanked Jeremy with all my heart for saving my life.

'You're not safe yet, John,' he said. '*I* know you're not an enemy of the King, but many people will not believe you. If you want to stay a free man and keep your farm and land, there's only one thing you can do – you must come to London with me and tell your story to Judge Jeffreys.'

—— 12 ——

Love and revenge

London, of course, was where Lorna was, but it was five weeks before I saw her. Because I was a kind of prisoner, I was not allowed to move freely around the city and I had to report every day to the judges' rooms. However, I came before Judge Jeffreys at last. He remembered me, believed my story, and gave me papers which said I was a free man and an honest servant of the King.

I was now free to go and see Lorna but, to tell the truth, I was a little afraid. It had been a year since she left Exmoor – a year without one word or letter from her. Did she remember the old days in our farmhouse? Did she still love her poor, simple farmer, a man without great riches or a famous family name? It was true that the Ridds had held their own land on Exmoor for hundreds of years, but Lorna came from a family that had Scottish kings in its history.

Everybody in London knew Lady Lorna Dugal. They spoke of her great beauty, and told me how rich she was, and that the Queen was very friendly with her. But if Lorna still loved me, then neither riches nor a proud family would keep me away from her.

So, with fear and hope in my heart, I went to Earl Brandir's house. It was a very grand place. I was taken upstairs to a little sitting-room, and told to wait. Then, suddenly, the door opened and Lorna was standing before me, in a simple white dress, with her long black hair falling down her back. She was more beautiful than ever.

She came towards me, holding out her hand. Gently, I took her hand in mine, then bent and kissed it.

'Is that all?' she whispered. I saw the shine of tears in her eyes, and in another second she was crying in my arms.

'Darling Lorna,' I cried, holding her close to me. 'I love

you dearly, but surely, you don't care for me now.'

'Yes, I do, John. Yes, I do. Oh, why have you behaved so unkindly?'

'I am behaving,' I replied, 'as well as I can. No other man in the world could hold you like this, without kissing you.'

'Then why don't you do it, John?' asked Lorna, looking up at me, with a laugh in her bright eyes.

After that, of course, there was no more talking, for about five minutes. Then my darling pulled away from me, and began to question me.

'John Ridd, you must tell me the truth, the whole truth. Why have you never, for more than a year, taken any notice of your old friend, Lorna Doone?'

'Because,' I answered, 'my old friend, and true love, sent me not one word or letter in all that time.'

'What!' cried Lorna. 'Oh no, my poor John! I have often suspected something like this, but she always said—' With these words, she rang a bell very violently, and a few seconds later her servant, little Gwenny, came in.

'Gwenny,' said Lorna, 'what have you done with all the letters I gave you to send to Mr Ridd? No more lies, now.'

Gwenny gave me a very black look. 'I didn't send them,' she said. 'You're a grand lady now, mistress. You should marry some grand lord, not a poor farmer from Exmoor. I was only thinking of you.'

'Gwenny, you may go,' said Lorna, her voice full of

Gwenny gave me a very black look.

quiet anger. 'I don't want to see you or speak to you for at least three days.'

At this, Gwenny ran out of the room, crying noisily, and Lorna turned to me. 'Oh John, try not to be too angry with her. She loves me very much, and I'm afraid that if you take me, you'll still have to take Gwenny too.'

'I'll take fifty Gwennies,' I said, 'if you want me to.'

After this, we spoke of ourselves. I tried to tell Lorna that, when she was free to decide her own future, she must think very carefully. The world would say she was mad if she chose to become a farmer's wife. Of course, at Plover's Barrows farm she would have a comfortable home, plenty of good food, and all the love and care I could give her. But it was not the same as being a grand lady, who owned half of Scotland and who could marry any lord she wanted.

Lorna could not wait for me to finish. 'I decided long ago, dear John,' she said, very seriously, 'that you must be my husband. I think it was the day you climbed up the waterfall, with your shoes off, and a bag of fish for your mother. So, after all these years of loving, shall little things like money and a family name separate us? They mean nothing. I have not been here a year, John, without learning something. Oh, how I hate it! Only my uncle and Gwenny really care for me. All the rest are only interested in my land and money. Oh John, you must never leave me – it would break my heart.'

Of course, I gave in at once, and said, 'Darling, you must do exactly what you please.'

For that she gave me the sweetest of kisses; and as I left, I went grandly down the great stairs of Earl Brandir's house, thinking of nothing else except that.

———— •◉• ————

For the rest of my time in London I went to see Lorna every day, forgetting all about my poor mother and the work that needed doing on the farm. Then one day I received a letter from Lizzie, and I realized that I must get home as quickly as possible. My darling Lorna cried and held me close, but she understood why I had to go.

Lizzie's news was this: Jeremy Stickles and his soldiers had finally made their attack on Doone valley – but it had failed, and Jeremy had been injured. This was the worst possible thing for Exmoor. Now the Doones would make more trouble than ever before – and of course they would attack our farm.

When I got home, I learnt that the Doones were robbing everyone around them, and the whole of Exmoor was living in fear of them. Then a few weeks later something even more terrible happened.

The Doones came one evening to the farmhouse of Kit Badcock, a neighbour of ours, while he was out working in his fields. They broke down the door and stole his young wife Margery. Two of them carried her, screaming and fighting, to their horses, and then rode away. Meanwhile, the other Doones were searching the house for food and drink to steal, and one of them found the Badcocks' little son crying in the kitchen. He picked the baby up, threw him into the air, and let him fall on to the hard stone floor. The child's neck was broken, and he died at once.

It made me sick just to think of the cruelty of this man, and when people heard this terrible story, they were very angry. They said it was time for the people of Exmoor to take their own revenge.

Men from all the farms and villages of Exmoor came to see me. 'We cannot expect any more help from the King against the Doones,' they told me. 'Because Jeremy Stickles's attack failed, the King has refused to send any more soldiers. But we've had enough of the Doones. We want to attack them ourselves, and we want you to lead us, John.'

I said I was no leader, but they would not listen to this.

'Try to lead us,' they said, 'and we will try to follow.'

In the end I agreed to do as they asked. I thought we had a chance against the Doones, if enough of us decided to fight. There were fewer of them now – some had been killed in the rebel fighting, and some during Jeremy's attack. We arranged to meet again and make a plan. Tom Faggus, now quite well, rode over to join us – and he soon had a very clever idea.

'We're not soldiers,' he said, 'and we'll never defeat the Doones if we try to fight all of them in their valley. So we must lay a trap. You know the caves on Exmoor where gold was once found? Well, we'll tell a story around Exmoor that men have been digging secretly and have found a new cave, with rocks full of gold. We'll say that the gold will be taken away on a certain night, at a certain time. The Doones will naturally plan to attack and steal this gold, but some of us will make a trap for them in the caves. Meanwhile, the rest of us will attack the valley, as soon as we know that some of the robbers have left.'

The second part of our plan was this: Tom would take some of our men and pretend to attack the Doone-gate, while our main attack would really come from the waterfall end of the valley – the route I had discovered so long ago.

The plan went well. The story about the gold was whispered in the right ears, and on the agreed night our spies watched a large group of robbers leave Doone valley on their way to the caves. Meanwhile, as the moon rose above the hills, I was leading my twenty men to the bottom of the waterfall. John Fry, our old farm-worker, was in the mountains which looked down into the valley. When he saw the fighting start at the Doone-gate, he would fire his gun as a signal to us.

Soon the sound of John's gun rang around the mountains, and I and my men climbed up the waterfall and into the valley. Tom's men were making as much noise as possible at the Doone-gate, and all the Doones had run to join the fight there. We went quietly along the valley, keeping to the shadows under the trees, until we came to the Doone-town. Then we got to work with our fire sticks, and before long every Doone house was on fire. We took good care, however, to burn no women or children, and we made sure that they were all out of the houses first.

When they saw the flames and smoke rising from their houses, the Doone men came running back from the gate. By the time they reached us, the whole valley was burning – houses, trees, everything, right up to the sides of the mountains. As the men came towards us, we saw that there were only twelve of them. In the bright firelight, they could not see us, but we had them right in front of our guns. There were so few of them that I thought we could take them as prisoners. But my men did not wait for a word from me – they saw the chance of revenge on the men who had burnt their homes and stolen their women for so many years. They fired, and five Doones fell dead.

The robbers fired back wildly, but they could not see us clearly in the shadows. Soon all the guns were empty, and

My men fired, and five Doones fell dead.

the battle became hand-to-hand fighting, with knives and
sticks. I stood to one side – the only Doone I wanted to
meet was Carver. But as I started to look for him, I saw
something white in the grass, moving close to the ground.
I ran to see what it was, and found the Counsellor. I
recognized him from Lorna's descriptions, and here he was,
on his hands and knees, trying to escape from the fighting.
The white thing I had seen was his long white hair. When
he saw me, he got to his feet. He knew at once who I was.

'John Ridd!' he said. 'Won't you be kind to an old man? Let me get away from this violence, John.'

'I will let you go free, sir,' I said, 'but on one condition. Tell me honestly, which Doone killed my father?'

'I will tell you honestly,' he said, 'though it hurts me to say it. It was my son, Carver.'

'I thought it was him,' I said. 'But you were not there, so I don't blame you.'

'I've always been against violence,' the Counsellor said, shaking his head sadly. 'And now, John, let me go.'

He was an evil, lying old man, but I let him go. I don't know what happened to him, but he was never seen again on Exmoor.

Then I went to look for Carver, but did not find him. Afterwards, I heard that he had led the Doones who had gone to the gold caves. Our trap was successful, and all the Doones had been killed – all except Carver, who had ridden his horse through the attackers and escaped.

The Doones were totally defeated, though. When the sun came up above their valley the next day, all their houses were nothing but blackened wood. We had lost sixteen men in the fighting, but out of nearly forty Doone men, only Carver and the Counsellor were left alive.

But the thought that Carver, that cruel and violent man, was still living somewhere on the moors, did not give me much peace.

— 13 —
The last battle

The next thing that happened was the return of Lorna – my Lorna, my own darling. She stepped out of her coach and ran into the house, as happy as a bird to get home again. All the house was full of brightness and sunshine as she ran here and there, laughing and talking. Oh, how she loved this old chair, and she must see the kitchen fire, and where was her old friend the cat? As for me, I threw my best hat over the hay ricks and shouted for happiness.

Lorna was now free to make her own decisions, she told us. Earl Brandir had died. She had grown to love this fine old gentleman, and was very sad at his death. But now she could do what she wanted – even marry that good servant of the King, John Ridd.

At last, the waiting and the worrying was over, and happiness was ours. But in her softest moments, when she was alone with me, Lorna could not quite hide the fear that still lay deep in her heart. I felt it too – a fear that something evil, something terrible, could still happen.

There was great excitement all over Exmoor when people heard of our wedding. Everyone had heard of the defeat of the Doones, and the strength of John Ridd, and the beauty of Lorna. People came from more than thirty miles around.

Mother, Annie, and Lizzie arranged everything, with the help of Uncle Ben's granddaughter, Ruth, who had also come for the wedding.

When the day came, and Lorna stepped up to my side in Oare church and took my hand, I was afraid to look at her. She was so beautiful, so fresh and lovely in her simple white dress. But when we had each said 'I will', and my ring was on her finger, we turned to each other. Her laughing eyes were serious now, and full of so much love that my heart nearly stopped beating. Darling eyes, the loveliest, the most loving eyes – then the sound of a shot rang through the church, and those eyes were clouded with death.

Lorna fell at my feet, and her bright red blood ran over the wooden floor. I lifted her up, whispering soft words of love, but as she leant her head on my chest, her eyes closed and she breathed her last goodbye to life. Then I laid my wife in my mother's arms – and went out for my revenge.

Of course, I knew who had done it. There was only one man in the world who could do a thing like this. I jumped on my horse and rode away fast. I don't remember who showed me the way. I only know that I took it. And the men fell back before me.

Soon the shouts of some men told me that I was getting close. And there, ahead of me, rode a man on a great black horse; and I knew that the man was Carver Doone.

'His life, or mine,' I said to myself; 'whatever God decides. But the two of us cannot live in this world one more hour together.' I had no weapons, and I knew he had a gun, but I also knew, as surely as night follows day,

I lifted her up, whispering soft words of love.

that I would kill this man.

He rode up onto the moors, and I followed. His horse was fast, but he did not know this part of Exmoor. He rode straight into a little valley from which I knew there was no escape – because at the end of it there was only a black, bottomless bog.

As I rode after him, I reached up to a tree that was growing in the rocks above me, and broke off a great branch. Then Carver turned a corner and saw what he was riding towards. He pulled back from the bog in fear, and turning his horse, he fired, and rode straight at me.

The bullet hit me somewhere, but I took no notice. I put my horse across his path, lifted the branch above my head and brought it down hard on his horse's head. Both horse and man crashed to the ground.

Before Carver could move, I jumped down. He got up with a black look on his face and started to speak. For an answer I hit him on the side of the face. I would not dirty my mouth by speaking to this man now. Then he ran at me and put his hands around my neck. I had never met strength like this, and felt my neck would break. But I took hold of his arm, and almost pulled it from his shoulder. Then I took him by the neck, as he had done to me. His eyes burned with anger, and he threw himself against me. But God gave me great strength that day. In two minutes he was lying on the ground, half dead.

'I will not hurt you any more,' I said, when I could breathe again. 'Carver Doone, you are beaten. Go on your way, thank God you are alive – and never come near me again.'

But it was too late. The black bog had him by the feet. As he lay like a mad dog in front of me, the ground itself began to pull him in. In our murderous battle, we had not noticed where we were going. I only just managed to jump, with my last strength, from the terrible blackness. But I could do nothing for Carver. While his mad eyes stared, and his arms waved wildly above his head, the black bog pulled him down and he disappeared from sight.

I don't know how I got home. I had lost a lot of blood. By the time I got to the farm, I was riding in a dream. John Fry took my horse away and Mother led me indoors.

'I have killed him,' I said, 'as he killed Lorna. Now let me see my wife. She belongs to me, though she is dead.'

'You cannot see her now, John,' said Ruth, coming forward. 'Annie is with her now.'

'What does that matter? Let me see my dead one, and then die.'

All the women moved away from me, crying. Only Ruth stood by me, and put her little hand in mine.

'John, she is not your dead one. She may still be your living one, and your wife. But you must not see her now. The sight of you like this will certainly kill her.'

I could not understand what she was saying, but I let them lead me upstairs to my bed. The bullet had broken a bone in my chest, and I was soon in a fever. It was only much later that I learnt how Ruth had saved Lorna's life.

The black bog pulled him down.

When I had run out of the church, Ruth had taken control. She made John Fry and the other men carry Lorna home immediately. There, she cut off the wedding dress, pulled the bullet from Lorna's wound, and stopped the bleeding with cold water. All this time, Lorna lay still and white, and everyone was sure that she would die.

71

But Ruth covered the wound with a cloth, kept her warm, and made her drink a little wine from a spoon. And after a while everyone could see that Lorna was still breathing. She lay close to death for many days, but with Ruth's loving care, she slowly began to get better.

Meanwhile, I lay in my bed, only half-conscious, and in my fever I did not believe them when they told me Lorna was still alive. I knew in my heart that she was dead, and I had no interest in life – a life without Lorna was worthless, without meaning.

Mother cried, and thought that I would die, but after six weeks the fever left me. I was so weak that I could not leave my room. Outside, the sun shone on the spring flowers, but in my misery I cared nothing for the beauty of the world.

Then, the next morning, Ruth came to see me. 'John,' she said, 'are you well enough to see your wife? I was afraid to bring her before, while you were so ill.'

'I don't understand,' I said, staring at her. She went away, then came back, and behind her was Lorna. Ruth closed the door, and ran away; and Lorna stood before me.

But she did not stand for long. She ran to me and managed to get into my arms, although they were too weak to hold her. She put her warm young face against mine, and would not look at me, preferring kissing to looking.

I felt my life come back to me. I felt the happiness of living, and of loving. I felt the sweetness and the sadness of my Lorna's tears, and the softness of her loving lips. And the world, suddenly, was a good place again.

———— •●• ————

I have not much more to tell. Over the days that followed, Lorna sat beside me, and we watched each other getting better. We have never tired of watching each other since.

Now, we live peacefully on the farm. Though Lorna still has great riches, we never use the money, except for some poor neighbour. I sometimes buy her beautiful clothes, but she soon gives them away, or keeps them for the children.

Tom and Annie are happy. Except for a few small adventures, Tom remains on the right side of the law, and they have honest children. Lizzie married the captain of Jeremy Stickles's soldiers, who had stayed with us when we fought the Doones. Ruth is not married yet, but there is a man who loves her, as much as I love Lorna, and I'm sure he will win her soon.

But of Lorna herself, my darling wife, I won't say much. A man should not talk too much about the best thing in his life. Year by year, her beauty and her loving kindness grow greater; and after all this time, and all that has happened to us, she is still my Lorna Doone.

GLOSSARY

attack *(v)* to start fighting someone or something; **attack** *(n)* an attempt to hurt someone or something

bog very soft, wet ground that pulls you down

darling a word for someone that you love very much

defend to fight to keep away dangerous things or people

earl a title for a man from a very grand family

evil very bad

fire *(v)* to shoot a gun

force *(v)* to make someone do something when they do not want to

gap an opening in something, or between two things

inn a house or small hotel where you can get meals and drinks, and a room for the night

lord a title for a man from an important family

master a man who has servants working for him

mistress a woman who has servants working for her

moor open, wild, high land

rebel a person who fights against his country's leaders

sand the soft, yellow or white earth that is found on beaches by the sea

signal a sign (e.g. a flag or a light) that sends a message to someone

size how big or small something is

strength being strong

Saint Valentine's Day February 14th; a day when lovers give each other cards and sometimes presents

tightly very closely and strongly

Lorna Doone

ACTIVITIES

Before Reading

1 Read the story introduction on the first page of the book, and the back cover. How much do you know now about the story? Are these sentences true (T) or false (F)?

1 Exmoor is a place where few people live. T/F

2 The Doones live on a hill on Exmoor. T/F

3 John comes from a family of farmers. T/F

4 John's father is shot while stealing from a farm. T/F

5 Lorna looks beautiful, but she is cold and proud. T/F

6 Two men want to marry Lorna Doone. T/F

2 Can you guess what will happen in the story? Choose answers to these questions.

1 Who will die?
   a) Lorna Doone   c) Carver Doone
   b) John Ridd   d) John Ridd's mother

2 Who will marry Lorna Doone?
   a) Carver Doone   c) Somebody else
   b) John Ridd   d) Nobody

3 What will happen to the Doones in the end?
   a) They will be caught and put in prison by the soldiers.
   b) They will move to another part of the country.
   c) They will continue to rob and murder on Exmoor.
   d) Most of them will be killed in a battle with Exmoor farmers.

While Reading

Read Chapters 1 and 2. Choose the best question-word for these questions, and then answer them.

What / Why

1 . . . did John remember the family in the coach?
2 . . . was the news at home that John didn't want to hear?
3 . . . didn't the local people fight back when the Doones attacked them?
4 . . . did John go looking for on Saint Valentine's Day?
5 . . . did John want to climb the waterfall?
6 . . . seemed to make Lorna sad?
7 . . . did Lorna tell John to go?

Read Chapters 3 to 5. Are these sentences true (T) or false (F)? Rewrite the false ones with the correct information.

1 Tom Faggus robbed the rich, but he never hurt anyone.
2 Uncle Ben did not see any way of attacking Doone valley.
3 When John saw Lorna again, he fell deeply in love.
4 Lorna could not remember her early childhood.
5 She told John that Carver Doone was kind and gentle, and she would be happy to marry him.
6 When John left, he promised to come back the next week.
7 Jeremy Stickles came to the farm to arrest John.
8 John thought London was an unpleasant place.
9 Judge Jeffreys sent John home to spy for the king.

Before you read Chapter 6 (*Lorna's new troubles*), what do you think those troubles will be? Choose some of these ideas.

1 The Doones try to force Lorna to promise that she will marry Carver.
2 Lorna's grandfather dies, and Lorna has to marry Carver.
3 John fights Carver Doone, and gets hurt.
4 The Doones find out about John's visits.
5 The Doones keep Lorna prisoner in her house.
6 Lorna has no way of getting a message to John.

Read Chapters 6 to 8. Who said this, and to whom? Who, or what, were they talking about?

1 'They say it's for the peace of the Doones.'
2 'I thought you were much too honest and simple ever to do something like this!'
3 'I was going mad, because I didn't know what had happened to you.'
4 'I'm afraid he won't live long.'
5 'I know she will love you with all her heart.'
6 'You must bring her here, and I will teach her how to be a farmer's wife.'
7 'We've been kept in here for days without food.'
8 'I shall wear it, my love, till the day I die.'
9 'It means that I am not a criminal any more.'
10 'I have been sent to do important work.'
11 'Ten of them, coming across the river. They'll be here in a minute.'
12 'I will kill any man who touches her.'

78

Read Chapters 9 to 11, and then answer these questions.

1 Who was Lorna, and what happened to her real parents?
2 Who was the 'old enemy' that Lorna's mother recognized?
3 In what way did the 'blackest and unhappiest' day of John's and Lorna's childhood join their lives together?
4 How did Lorna feel about marrying a simple farmer now?
5 Why did the Doones never tell Lorna who she really was?
6 Why did Lorna have to go to London?
7 Why did John think Lorna had forgotten about him?
8 How did John help Tom Faggus?
9 Why was John so pleased to see Jeremy Stickles again?

Before you read Chapters 12 and 13, how do you think the story ends? Choose some of these ideas.

1 John finds Lorna in London, and she still loves him.
2 Earl Brandir refuses to allow Lorna to marry John.
3 Lorna has married a rich lord, but runs away with John.
4 Jeremy Stickles and his soldiers attack Doone valley.
5 John leads the Exmoor people in an attack on the Doones.
6 The Doones' houses are burnt and all the men die in the fires.
7 All the Doones are killed except Carver and his father.
8 John marries Lorna and goes to live in London.
9 Carver Doone shoots Lorna at the wedding and kills her.
10 Carver shoots John, who nearly dies from his wound.
11 John fights Carver to the death and breaks his neck.
12 After a terrible fight, John watches Carver die.
13 The story ends happily.

After Reading

1 Here is Ruth, writing about the day of the wedding in her diary. Put the parts of sentences in the right order, and join them with these linking words to make a passage of seven sentences. Start with number 10.

after / and / and / and after / because / but / however / so /
when / where

1 badly wounded from his fight with Carver,

2 _____ we heard the sound of Carver's gun in the church.

3 _____ at last he realized that his wife was alive and well.

4 I told the men to carry Lorna home.

5 _____ in his fever the poor man did not believe us.

6 I managed to make her drink a little wine.

7 _____ we put him to bed too,

8 _____ I took Lorna to see him for the first time,

9 There, I cut off her wedding dress, took out the bullet,

10 It was a terrible moment

11 _____ he lay in a fever for several weeks.

12 Today, he is the happiest man on earth,

13 _____ John had run out to chase Carver,

14 _____ yesterday John's fever left him.

15 We told him many times that Lorna was still alive,

16 Then John arrived home,

17 _____ I had stopped the bleeding,

18 Slowly, _____, both he and Lorna began to get better,

2 Perhaps this is what some of the characters in the story were thinking. Which six characters were they, and what was happening in the story at that moment?

1 'She's a lovely girl, and we're very happy together, but oh! life on the farm is so *boring*! And just a few hours away there's excitement, and fighting, and adventure . . . It's no use, I *have* to go . . .'

2 'What on earth is he thinking of? In love with a Doone! The family that killed his father! I don't know whether to cry, or hit him, or go away from here right now . . .'

3 'It's just not right! She's a lady now, with grand friends – why is she still writing to that rough farmer? Well, I'll have nothing to do with it – I'm going to hide this one too . . .'

4 'I'll have to tell him now, but I don't think he's going to like it. He's a good, honest man, but he's only a simple farmer, and when this news gets out, that young lady will be able to marry any man in the country . . .'

5 'I'll make him sorry that he pulled my beard! He won the battle tonight, but I'll be back. And then *he'll* be on his knees in front of *me*! Lorna belongs to me, and nobody – *nobody* is going to keep her from me . . .'

6 'He's certainly big and strong, that young man. And he looks me straight in the eye when he answers a question. I like that. But a spy? I don't think so. He's too honest – you can read his face like a book . . .'

3 There are 18 words from the story hidden in this word search. Find the words and draw lines through them. The first and last letters of each word are given below, and the words go from left to right and from top to bottom.

A____K	D____D	M____R	S____D	V____Y
B____G	F____E	N____T	S____L	W____L
C____H	G____P	R____L	S____M	
D____G	I____N	S____D	S____Y	

I	N	N	H	S	I	G	N	A	L
N	E	S	T	I	S	L	I	S	F
W	A	T	E	R	F	A	L	L	D
E	O	R	R	M	I	N	E	E	E
D	R	E	B	E	L	W	H	D	F
A	A	A	C	B	T	F	I	R	E
R	E	M	O	O	R	V	E	R	N
L	G	O	A	G	D	S	A	N	D
I	D	S	C	E	C	G	A	P	I
N	D	P	H	A	T	T	A	C	K
G	E	Y	S	V	A	L	L	E	Y

Now write down all the letters that don't have a line through them (begin with the first line and go across each line until the end). You will have 31 letters, which make a sentence of 7 words.

1 What is the sentence?
2 Who said it, and to whom?
3 What did happen, in the end?

82

4 **Complete this letter from Jeremy Stickles to Judge Jeffreys, using the words below.**

broke, broken, buried, burning, defeated, farm, have, living, lost, ordered, others, ring, sign, towards, uncle, waiting

The Doones attacked John Ridd's _____ last night, but Ridd and I were _____ for them. Two of them went _____ the hay ricks with _____ sticks, and Ridd caught them and _____ their arms. Then I _____ my men to fire. We killed two men, and the _____ ran. We _____ the dead men today, and I sent the two men with _____ arms to Taunton. Ridd told me it was the first time the Doones had ever been _____.

Young Lorna Doone is now _____ with the Ridds, but I _____ discovered that she is not a Doone at all, but the _____ daughter of Lord Dugal. She has an old family _____, with the _____ of the House of Lorne on it. I expect her _____, Earl Brandir, will be interested in this news.

5 **Imagine that you could give the story a different ending. Choose one of the endings below and write the notes into a paragraph. Then say which ending you prefer, and why.**

- Lorna married / lord in London (Was John sad all his life? Did he forget Lorna / marry an Exmoor girl?)
- Lorna died / John / unhappy (Did he ever marry again?)
- John and Lorna married / lived in London (How did John feel about living in London?)
- Carver escaped from the bog (Did he leave the country / become a good man / make his peace with John?)

ABOUT THE AUTHOR

Richard Doddridge Blackmore was born in 1825. Like John Ridd in the story, he went to school in Tiverton; later he went to Oxford University, and then worked as a lawyer and a teacher. His health was poor, however, and when he inherited some money, he built a house near London and made his living from gardening and writing. He was a very shy and secretive man, whose great pleasure was his garden, full of rare plants; he was especially proud of his peaches, which were not common in England then. He died in 1900.

Although he wrote only a page a day, he produced fourteen novels and several other books. The success of *Lorna Doone* was at first due to a mistake: when it came out in 1869, one of Queen Victoria's daughters had just married the Marquis of Lorne, and people bought the book because they thought it was about the Marquis's family. In fact, there was no connection, but the novel became very popular and remains so today.

Blackmore used to hear tales about the land and people of Exmoor from his grandfather, who had been rector of Oare. He used these when he was writing *Lorna Doone*, and he based the characters of John Ridd and Tom Faggus on people who lived at the time. And this is how Blackmore himself was described by his publisher: 'He was very tall, and of a large muscular frame . . . he dressed very plainly . . . his voice was gentle and yet manly.' It could be John Ridd himself.

Lorna Doone has been filmed, most recently in 1993, and the wild and beautiful Doone Valley on Exmoor still attracts thousands of visitors each year.

OXFORD BOOKWORMS LIBRARY

Classics • Crime & Mystery • Factfiles • Fantasy & Horror
Human Interest • Playscripts • Thriller & Adventure
True Stories • World Stories

The OXFORD BOOKWORMS LIBRARY provides enjoyable reading in English, with a wide range of classic and modern fiction, non-fiction, and plays. It includes original and adapted texts in seven carefully graded language stages, which take learners from beginner to advanced level. An overview is given on the next pages.

All Stage 1 titles are available as audio recordings, as well as over eighty other titles from Starter to Stage 6. All Starters and many titles at Stages 1 to 4 are specially recommended for younger learners. Every Bookworm is illustrated, and Starters and Factfiles have full-colour illustrations.

The OXFORD BOOKWORMS LIBRARY also offers extensive support. Each book contains an introduction to the story, notes about the author, a glossary, and activities. Additional resources include tests and worksheets, and answers for these and for the activities in the books. There is advice on running a class library, using audio recordings, and the many ways of using Oxford Bookworms in reading programmes. Resource materials are available on the website <www.oup.com/elt/bookworms>.

The *Oxford Bookworms Collection* is a series for advanced learners. It consists of volumes of short stories by well-known authors, both classic and modern. Texts are not abridged or adapted in any way, but carefully selected to be accessible to the advanced student.

You can find details and a full list of titles in the *Oxford Bookworms Library Catalogue* and *Oxford English Language Teaching Catalogues*, and on the website <www.oup.com/elt/bookworms>.

STARTER • 250 HEADWORDS

present simple – present continuous – imperative –
can/cannot, must – *going to* (future) – simple gerunds ...

Her phone is ringing – but where is it?

Sally gets out of bed and looks in her bag. No phone. She looks under the bed. No phone. Then she looks behind the door. There is her phone. Sally picks up her phone and answers it. *Sally's Phone*

STAGE 1 • 400 HEADWORDS

... past simple – coordination with *and, but, or* –
subordination with *before, after, when, because, so* ...

I knew him in Persia. He was a famous builder and I worked with him there. For a time I was his friend, but not for long. When he came to Paris, I came after him – I wanted to watch him. He was a very clever, very dangerous man. *The Phantom of the Opera*

STAGE 2 • 700 HEADWORDS

... present perfect – *will* (future) – *(don't) have to, must not, could* –
comparison of adjectives – simple *if* clauses – past continuous –
tag questions – *ask/tell* + infinitive ...

While I was writing these words in my diary, I decided what to do. I must try to escape. I shall try to get down the wall outside. The window is high above the ground, but I have to try. I shall take some of the gold with me – if I escape, perhaps it will be helpful later. *Dracula*

Of course, it was most important that no one should see Colin, Mary, or Dickon entering the secret garden. So Colin gave orders to the gardeners that they must all keep away from that part of the garden in future. *The Secret Garden*

... past perfect continuous – passive (simple forms) –
would conditional clauses – indirect questions –
relatives with *where/when* – gerunds after prepositions/phrases ...

I was glad. Now Hyde could not show his face to the world again. If he did, every honest man in London would be proud to report him to the police. *Dr Jekyll and Mr Hyde*

... future continuous – future perfect –
passive (modals, continuous forms) –
would have conditional clauses – modals + perfect infinitive ...

If he had spoken Estella's name, I would have hit him. I was so angry with him, and so depressed about my future, that I could not eat the breakfast. Instead I went straight to the old house. *Great Expectations*

When I stepped up to the piano, I was confident. It was as if I knew that the prodigy side of me really did exist. And when I started to play, I was so caught up in how lovely I looked that I didn't worry how I would sound. *The Joy Luck Club*

Little Women

LOUISA MAY ALCOTT

Retold by John Escott

When Christmas comes for the four March girls, there is no money for expensive presents and they give away their Christmas breakfast to a poor family. But there are no happier girls in America than Meg, Jo, Beth, and Amy. They miss their father, of course, who is away at the Civil War, but they try hard to be good so that he will be proud of his 'little women' when he comes home.

This heart-warming story of family life has been popular for more than a hundred years.

Silas Marner

GEORGE ELIOT

Retold by Clare West

In a hole under the floorboards Silas Marner the linen-weaver keeps his gold. Every day he works hard at his weaving, and every night he takes the gold out and holds the bright coins lovingly, feeling them and counting them again and again. The villagers are afraid of him and he has no family, no friends. Only the gold is his friend, his delight, his reason for living.

But what if a thief should come in the night and take his gold away? What will Silas do then? What could possibly comfort him for the loss of his only friend?